YOU SHOULD WANT THIS HUG

The Benefits of a Hug

By

Gwendolyn B. Elmore

Published by Truly In His Hands March 2021

This book contains personal stories of others benefiting from hugs. Studies from Trusted Sources are included and have been given credit. It also includes information given by the Mayo Clinic and was reproduced with their permission. It may also contains charts and illustrations found on Healthline and other sites that encourage us to live healthy lifestyles.

The anonymous quotes used were found and no one had taken ownership of these quotes.

Holy Bible King James Bible, NIV, ERV, AMP

Strong Concordance 1993

ISBN 978-0-9897328-3-3

Printed in the United States of America

This book is being dedicated to all the people who have always expressed and experienced the good feeling of hugging but have not known the benefits of giving and receiving a good hug.

The past year, March 2020 – present has as we are living time of social distancing and many are being deprived of giving and receiving hugs, how unfortunate that is for many. Hugs boost your immune system; a healthy immune system can fight off any disease that challenges the body.

I pray you find comfort in knowing how we have been designed with the ability for our bodies to heal itself.

"You Should Want This Hug" is a book written to assist others with understanding the benefits of a hug. There are so many emotions that we feel when we embrace or hug.

Enjoy this read.

One of the greatest things about giving a hug is that in the process you too can receive a hug back. Do you know that feeling when you receive a hug after getting some bad news? The calming feeling of a touch lowers your blood pressure. Hugs give us so many health benefits and we should always want to give and receive them.

The definition of hug is to keep close to; as, to hug the land; to hug the wind. 6. (n.) A close embrace or clasping with the arms, as in affection or in wrestling. Strong Number Greek 1723. enagkalizomai -- to take into one's arms, to embrace. Hugs have been around for as long as people have been a part of this world and possible before. Have yo ever experienced a hug from God? Some of you are probably saying, "How is that even physically possible?" "A hug from God?" come on Elmore you are really stretching it. Take a moment to really think about it. There have been times when you have felt loved, you felt safe and you have felt a presence and there wasn't anyone else in the room but you. That feeling of peace while you were going through something that had you crying so hard you thought you would fall apart. You have felt it before.... Do you remember?

God does give hugs and you have probably experienced it and all you knew was that you were the only person visible but after receiving it you felt so much better. Think about how you feel when you see someone you love and care about so much, hurting. What is your first response? We are made in the image of God and his first response to us is showing us love and compassion, why would our response be any different. Even when we meet strangers and they tell us something about their lives that was painful, we offer hugs to console them. Our Creator, our Father, Prince of Peace and Holy Spirit, our Comforter is no different. When God said, let us make man, who do you think He was talking to? Our life experiences have caused some of us to lose the compassion that is already in us. When we cannot express it, it is only because we have allowed pain from our past to affect how we respond to others. The problems many has made many of us bitter and that is not the original plan for man. Now that we have an idea of why our response is different, let us make an effort to work on it.

What instructions our Creator given to us in our daily manual for our lives? We should begin by asking for a clean heart to be created in us.

Create in me a clean heart, O God, And renew a steadfast spirit within me.

Psalm 51:10

This next sentence that I read in an article at knowing.jesus.com took this scripture to another level for me.

"The corrupted gene-pool from our first sinning parents has been passed down the generations of humankind for six-thousand long years, resulting in defilement, disease, and death." (knowingjesus.com)

3

This gave me a much better view on why we could continue to have a problem. Reading that sentence helped me better understand the struggle for some because it has already been imbedded but it is totally up to us not to allow it to affect us in a negative way.

God, create a pure heart in me, and make my spirit strong again.

Psalm 51:10 ERV

Create in me a pure heart, O God. Renew an unwavering spirit within me.

Psalm 51:10 EHV

What we think and how we feel about others is how we respond to each other. We can use Philippians 4:8 for our daily meditation to ensure that we are thinking good thoughts about ourselves and about others.

Finally, believers, whatever is true, whatever is honorable and worthy of respect, whatever is right and confirmed by God's word, whatever is pure and wholesome, whatever is lovely and brings peace, whatever is admirable and of good repute; if there is any excellence, if there is anything worthy of praise, think continually on these things [center your mind on them, and implant them in your heart]. Philippians 4:8 AMP

For the rest, brethren, whatever is true, whatever is worthy of reverence and is honorable and seemly, whatever is just, whatever is pure, whatever is lovely and lovable, whatever is kind and winsome and gracious, if there is any virtue and excellence, if there is anything worthy of praise, think on and weigh and take account of these things [fix your minds on them].

Philippians 4:8 AMP

"Let his left hand be under my head And his right hand embrace me."

Song of Solomon 2:6 AMP

[I can feel] his left hand under my head and his right hand embraces me!

Song of Solomon 2:6 AMPC

Other scriptures you can research about holy kisses

II Corinthians 13:12

Genesis 28:6

Mark 10:16

Isaiah 66:13

Ecclesiastes 3:5

Hugs Were A Part of Daily Living for Us

Growing up in a household where hugs were given everyday and often. Our family was always loving and affectionate. Our father's side of the family were always hugging us and each other. Our paternal grandmother, Maggie Singletary Frazier Howell, gave great hugs all the time. And so that was the tradition for all of uncles, aunts and cousins and continues today. Our Daddy, Dr. Patrick Frazier, Sr. expressed that our hugs needed to matter to the ones receiving them. "Hug them with care so they can feel it", is what comes to mind."

Not everyone likes to receive hugs. It was not until my adult life when I realized that there were many people who did not appreciate being hugged. I encounter many who were not receptive to receiving hugs. Was them not wanting the hug supposed to stop me from walking in obedience? Well so happen these were individuals who attended worship services where I attended at the time so they could not get away.

Remembering now how some of them told me that they did not like that I was giving them hugs but soon discovered that they began to look forward to seeing me to receive one. They said there was something different about the hugs I gave, they felt a sense of peace but tried to fight it because they were not accustomed to receiving them growing. It was then I learned that the hugs that were received from me was more than just hugs.

I remember feelings of releasing a spirit of peace that I did not quite understand early on. As time went on, I was impressed to embrace selective individuals. There were times when I would be in the store shopping or even riding in the car and would feel impressed to hug a random individual. This was something that my husband was hesitate about me doing but as he began to discern what was happening, then he was able to fully support my actions. Those individuals began to share stories/testimonies of them feeling much better after receiving a hug from me. There are times when I was impressed in my spirit to give total strangers not a hug but a word of encouragement about something that they knew I could have any way of knowing. Now that...okay you know, I did not want to be known the "spooky one". LOL

HUGS CAN PUT A SMILE ON YOUR FACE

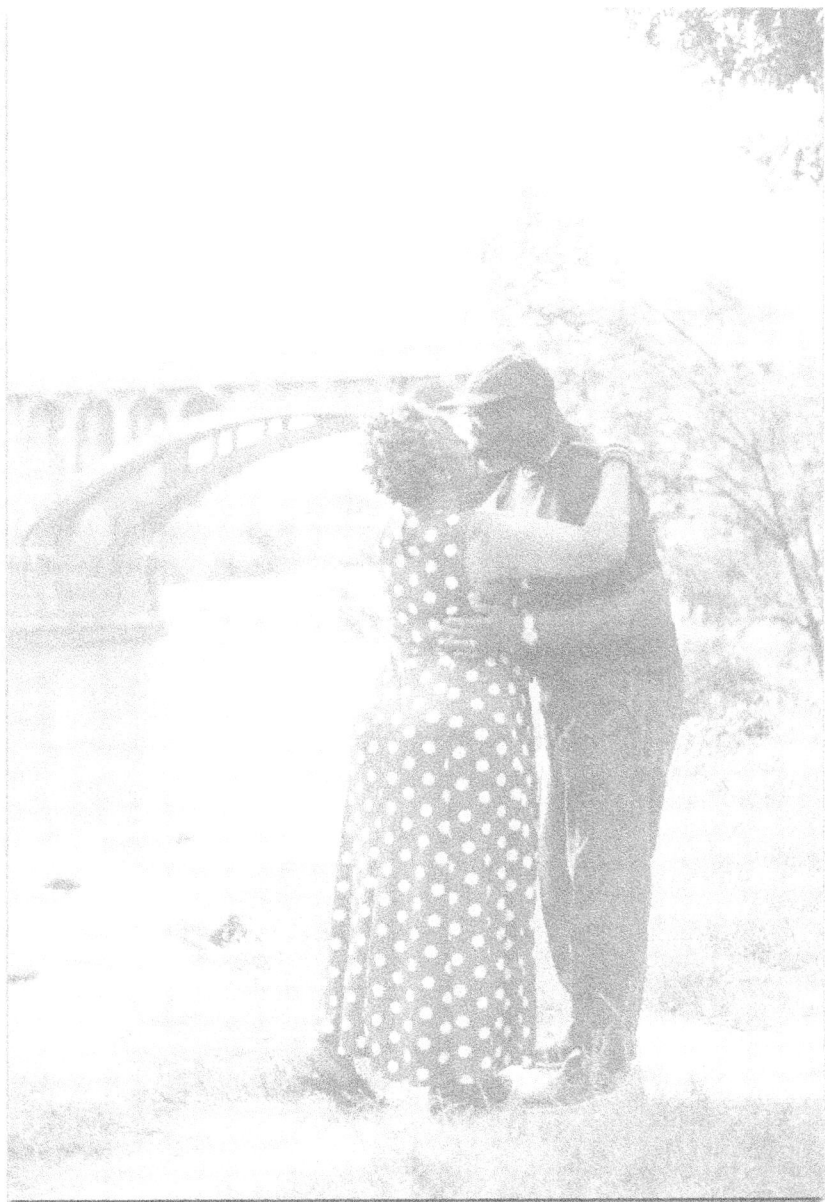

Statements made about my hugs:

"I get the feeling of how a child should feel from a mother's hug."

"You give the BEST hugs; I look forward to seeing you every week at service to get your hugs"

"I just want to lay out everything I did wrong and tell you about it."

"You always hug like you care and I just sat back and had to test you. I would compare the hug I got the last time from you and let me tell you it is always the same, a genuine hug."

I have people to come and bring others to meet me just so they could feel what it felt like to receive a genuine hug.

I want readers to walk away understanding how important it is to give and receive hugs as often as possible. Ideally it would be nice to start at home with your spouse and children if you all already have a good relationship. Good hugs are being promoted here and understand that if a hug does not feel good in the sense that you feel safe when you receive it and not troubled. Understand that safe, healthy hugs are those that help boost your immune system.

Please take time to read this book with your spouse and family as often as you can, so that you all can go and grow in your relationships. Pass it on to your grandchildren and those who you meet.

The very thing that is best for you during this time, is being discouraged. There is healing power in touch.

One of the most interesting effects of the hug is it's ability to lower blood pressure and heart rate. Of course, there are a number of medical reasons for this, and it is simply one more reason to enjoy a friendly hug. When a person is hugged, their comfort level is increased, and they enjoy being around a fellow human being. Also, the hug communicates many things to many people. A hug from a friend or family brings back happy memories and makes the huggee relive those moments. Also, if we follow social psychology, we become aware of the many benefits that result in the body and mind when we feel accepted or understood by another person. Even though one may think that a deep conversation can have these effects, the simple truth is that a hug creates those feelings of acceptance and compassion that can sometimes be difficult to find in our modern world. Thus, when we experience these things, we become more relaxed, we are happier, and our entire attitude tends to improve. As a direct result of these things, our heart rates become more relaxed and over a period, lower heart rates and increased time spent being happy can actually lower blood pressure and have very effective bonuses to heart health.

Even though benefits relating to lower heart rate and blood pressure may seem obvious when we explore them, one interesting fact that not many are aware of is that hugs are sometimes used as a form of physical therapy. Think about it: when you give or receive a hug, you are making full body contact with another person. Medical science has shown and proven that contact of this kind can stimulate nerve endings throughout the body and increase circulation. Thus, some physical rehabilitation centers use hugs of various kinds in order to stimulate nerve endings and increase blood flow throughout the body. It is a simple side effect, but one that can make a major difference when speaking about overall body health.

Another important benefit of the hug is the effect that it can on the mental state of an individual, as well as the physical. People who hug more frequently tend to be more open about their emotions and develop a greater sense of closeness and compassion to those around them. However, sometimes, it can be difficult to accept others or to realize that there are other people around us. For that reason, sometimes the simple hug can open up mental blocks with this matter, allowing an individual to feel increased feelings of happiness and even trigger a small release of dopamine. However, even though physical contact can sometimes have brain chemical effects (such as the release of dopamine mentioned before) it is not a constant. Instead, the greater benefits in this area come from the simple effect of being close to other human beings and feeling a real bond or connection between people.

So, even though we may not often think about the hug as a way to improve our health and improve the day and life of someone else, it can often have this effect. And, after all, what better way to celebrate Valentines' Day than with a friendly hug. Of course, remember that not everyone likes to be hugged, and always ask before giving a hug to someone who you may not be sure wants a hug. In closing, remember the simple things in life that can make such a difference, and the hug is definitely one of them.

Hugging is an extremely positive form of communication. It expresses the values of love, approval, gratitude, and forgiveness. Hugging is a great form of emotional satisfaction, but it also has some surprising health benefits. In this article we will share with you the health benefits of hugging – the ones you probably haven´t thought about. -Urmet Seepter-

THERE ARE DIFFERENT TYPES OF HUGS. WHICH ONES ARE YOUR FAVORITES?

TYPES OF HUGS

1. Around the waist

2. The quick pat

3. The Slow Dance

4. The strong hug

5. The hug with head on shoulder

6. The bear hug

7. The romantic hug between couples

8. The friendly hug between friends

9. The Polite hug

10. The Bear kind of hug

11. The Unreciprocated hug (no return)

12. The Squeeze hug

13. The Snuggle Type hug

14. The Buddy hug

Just to name a few

SEVEN BENEFITS OF HUGGING

7 Benefits of Hugging

1. Reduces heart disease

2. Diminishes stress

3. Promotes longevity

4. Strengthens social ties

5. Lowers blood pressure

6. Lowers heart rate

7. Benefits the hugger and the huggee equally

People are forgetting what love means nowadays. They stopped hugging, kissing and showing affection to each other. By doing this they start leading life that is empty and that brings sadness.

Hugs are the most natural way to show love, affection, understanding or comfort to someone. Sincere hug will show someone that you care about him or her. By hugging someone you will say hello and you will accept someone.

Juan Mann is a man that started with an interesting project called "free hugs". This project can help anyone who is lonely to feel good again.

Hugging is a powerful way to get rid of stress and to connect with people. It is our natural urge to love and connect to each other. By giving free hugs you will make anyone's day.

Research has been conducted showing that hugs produce oxytocin, a "bonding" hormone. Oxytocin influences social recognition, bonding, and building trust among people. By hugging we lower cortisol, the stress hormone. Cortisol is responsible for high blood pressure and slowing of metabolism. Combination of these two leads to gaining weight.

Dr. Charmaine Griffiths claims that people who are supported, loved and hugged by loved ones stand better chances to prevent or cure all illnesses connected with heart.

Dr. Karen Grewen said that hugging and showing affection are beneficial for all people, especially women. Hugging increases level of oxytocin bringing emotional stability and physical health.

A study from UNC-Chapel Hill was conducted on 100 adults showing that hugging protects heart from damaging influence of anger.

David Bresler did an amazing test on a woman who suffered from different types of pain in the body. After her husband gave her four hugs every day, her physical condition started improving.

Dr. Dolores Krieger proved that when we touch each other, and especially when we hug, we increase the production of hemoglobin which brings oxygen throughout our entire body. In this way we feel that we are healthy and full of energy.

In order to benefit from hugs these hugs need to be open and sincere.If we give A-frame hug, half-hug, chest-to-chest burp, wallet-rub, jock-twirl and similar imitations of true, warm hugging, we show nothing but fear from each other. This will not leave positive impact on our health.

A real hug includes whole body. In this way you protect your heart, feel younger and fit and maintain friendships and love with people. If you hug every day, you will simply feel happy. Do not be afraid of people, relax and hug as many people as possible.

This and other forms of physical touch is shown in research to stimulate the release three specific neurotransmitters in the brain: Dopamine, Serotonin, and Oxytocin. Dopamine is responsible for the feelings of pleasure, warmth and reward. Dopamine is the central neurotransmitter that gets released in many addictions, including food, sex, and drug additions. Serotonin is responsible for elevating mood, alleviating anxiety and decreasing feelings of loneliness. Oxytocin (also known as the cuddle hormone) increases social adhesion, encourages bonding, and increases feelings of trust with that person who you are connecting. The release of these neurotransmitters from the brain decreases stress, fear, and pain, decreases heart rate and breathing rate, and even lowers blood pressure.

Hugs cause the release of oxytocin in the brain. Oxytocin is commonly known as the cuddle hormone and elevates the mood. So, get 12 hugs today. In fact, get 12 hugs every day this week and see how it affects your overall moods & the moods of those you hug. Of course, be appropriate in the distribution of your hugs, for some you may need to give them notice or ask permission.

"A good hug speaks directly to your body and soul, making you feel loved and special," says Mihalko Baczynski, a relationship coach.

"Hugging is all natural; it is organic, naturally sweet, no pesticides, non-fattening, no carbohydrates, no preservatives, no artificial or genetically engineered ingredients, and 100% wholesome" says Dorothy M. Neddermeyer, PhD.

Not only are hugs completely natural, they don't cost anything either! Hugs are free! And best of all, the supply is endless.

Several sources suggest that everyone needs at least four hugs a day for healthy survival, eight hugs a day for emotional strength, and 12 hugs a day to really grow and be empowered. Stop and think about just how often you give or get a hug.

Start by giving your love a healthy hug today. Include more hugs in your daily routine. Ask yourself whose day could I improve by giving them one or more hugs today? Not only will you be helping them, but you'll benefit too.

Some people don't like their personal space to be invaded. Others may feel too vulnerable at times to want to be touched. So proceed with caution if you feel this way or if you sense discomfort in someone else. For some people, it may take a bit of getting used to

8 Hugs A Day for Better Health!

Yes! Who would have thought? By giving eight to twelve hugs a day, you are improving your health!

The healing hormone responsible for this is oxytocin, also known as the "bonding hormone". By physically touching someone you care about, such as giving a hug, the levels of oxytocin made by your brain, markedly rise. This causes you – and the person you hugged – to feel calm, happier and more connected as well as producing other health benefits.

Oxytocin has long been known as the "pair bonding" hormone and the "cuddle" hormone for its effect on stable monogamous relationships. As an Ob/Gyn, I have been very familiar with the role of oxytocin in childbirth, allowing for uterine contractions and the birth of a baby, as well as breast-feeding with milk "let-down".

Initial research in early 1990's found that breastfeeding women tended to have lower blood pressure. Lactation is a time when huge amounts of oxytocin are released from the brain to the breast tissue allowing milk to flow. The connection between decreased blood pressure and oxytocin then led to further investigation into its breadth and healing power. Oxytocin receptors have now been identified in other tissues, including the heart, kidney, thymus, and pancreas.

New exciting research has shown that oxytocin can play a powerful role in protecting your heart. By touching another person, oxytocin is produced in your heart and travels throughout your blood vessels dilating them through a mechanism of increased nitric oxide. (Not nitrous oxide, which is laughing gas!) Nitric oxide dilates our blood vessels, leading to a decrease in blood pressure, less inflammation, and less plaque build-up. Excess chronic inflammation is the key player in plaque buildup in our arteries, known as atherosclerosis. Oxytocin has been shown to reduce free radical formation and other inflammatory markers decreasing the risk for heart attack.

REMINDER:

BOOST YOUR IMMUNE SYSTEM

20 SECOND HUGS FOR YOU HEALTH

In an article was written by Lauren Sharkey, explains why touch is important.

Why is touch important?

Skin-to-skin contact is vital not only for mental and emotional health but physical health, too.

When you feel snowed under or pressured, the body releases the stress hormone cortisol. One of the biggest things touch can do is reduce such stress, allowing the immune system to work the way it should.

Touch can also calm certain bodily functions as written by Trusted Source, such as your heart rate and blood pressure.

It does so by stimulating pressure receptors, as written by a Trusted Source, that transport signals to the vagus nerve (each of the tenth pair of cranial nerves, supplying the heart, lung

s, upper digestive tract, and other organs of the chest and abdomen.). This nerve connects the brain to the rest of the body. It uses the signals to slow the pace of the nervous system.

In early life, touch is thought to be crucial for building healthy relationships by stimulating pathways for oxytocin, the natural antidepressant serotonin, and the pleasure neurotransmitter dopamine.

Plus, it can tackle loneliness. According to a 2017 study Trusted Source, gentle touch can reduce both pain and feelings of social exclusion.

How do you know if you're touch starved?

There's no definitive way to know. But in a nutshell, you may feel overwhelmingly lonely or deprived of affection.

These symptoms may be combined with:

1. feelings of depression
2. anxiety
3. stress
4. low relationship satisfaction
5. difficulty sleeping
6. a tendency to avoid secure attachments.

You may also subconsciously do things to simulate touch, such as taking long, hot baths or showers, wrapping up in blankets, and even holding on to a pet.

What if you don't particularly like being touched — can you still be touch starved?

Some people closely link touch with trust. If they don't trust a person, they're unlikely to want that person to touch them. But that doesn't mean they don't long for the benefits of a hug or handshake.

For example, not liking touch is sometimes reported by people on the neurodiverse spectrum and people who are asexual.

It may also be a result of childhood experiences. A 2012 study suggests that people whose parents were regular huggers were more likely to hug people in adulthood.

Failing to experience frequent positive touch as a child may affect the development of the oxytocin system

Trusted Source and the child's intimacy and social skills — although this isn't true for everyone.

What can you do to help satiate this desire?

Touch starvation does not have to last forever.

Here are some simple ways to welcome more affection into your life right now.

Keep in mind you may need to dial these activities back a bit during the COVID-19 pandemic, or avoid them until your local health officials give the OK:

Try out a massage. Whether you ask a loved one or visit a professional, massages can help you relax and enjoy the benefits of another person's touch.

Spend some quality time with animals. Often all too happy to cuddle, pets are the ideal soothing mechanism. According to the Centers for Disease Control and Prevention (CDC)Trusted Source, the risk of animals transmitting the coronavirus to people is low, based on limited information currently available.

Get your nails done. A manicure or pedicure may give you the human contact you need, and a new look to boot. When your local health department gives the OK, think about dressing up your hands and feet.

Visit the hair salon. If you don't fancy a cut, book yourself a wash and blow-dry for ultimate relaxation.

Learn to dance. Most slow dances are built around skin-to-skin contact. That may not be a good choice during the pandemic. But as soon as you're vaccinated and your health department gives a thumbs-up, think about learning some new moves.

Go to a cuddle party. Yes, these are real. And no, they're not as strange as they sound. As soon as you and your friends are vaccinated and your health department gives the go-ahead for indoor gatherings, consider trying it out.

What can you do to encourage affectionate touch in your day to day? With lockdowns, closed businesses, and medical advice to physically distance and avoid touching people not in your household, human touch has dwindled to a slow stream. For some, it has dried up altogether.

Medical facilities like the Department of Psychiatry and Behavioral Sciences at the University of California, San Francisco and the Texas Medical Center warn that touch starvation is real. It's important to find ways to keep in touch during the pandemic. Sustaining regular touch during the COVID-19 pandemic can be challenging. If you live with other people or are part of a pod, there are likely people you can touch safely. You might try the tips below.

For yourself

Sit close to your loved ones. Instead of spreading out on the couch, make an effort to cuddle up during your Netflix sprees.

Greet household members with a hug. If hugging people within your household or pod is safe, try this type of greeting. It may help both of you satisfy your touch hunger.

Use touch when appropriate. In a romantic relationship, hold hands or cuddle. In platonic ones, reassure people with a touch to the arm or a pat on the back. Always make sure the touch is safe and other people are comfortable before going ahead.

For your loved ones

Give them plenty of positive touch. This can range from gentle strokes to full-on cuddling a few times a day.

Avoid associating touch with negativity. Don't pinch or push or do anything that takes away the feel-good vibes of physical contact.

Let children be close to you as often as possible. Allowing your child to sit on your lap or gently massaging your baby are important for bonding and the emotional growth of the child.

If you can't touch safely

Maybe you're one of the 35.7 million Americans who live alone. Or maybe you live with people who work in high-risk settings. Or perhaps touch in pandemic circumstances just is not worth the risk to you.

In these and countless other scenarios, you may not have the opportunity for touch, or you may not feel safe with any human touch right now. There are still ways you can help satisfy your touch hunger — without physical contact.

Try the tips below. They might not be the real thing, but they do provide human contact and interaction:

Meet new people or connect with friends online. Technology provides many ways for online contact. Try video chat or virtual exercise classes or book clubs.

Wave to neighbors or passersby. Most of us take a daily walk. Try waving and maybe even meeting new people, from a physical distance, of course.

Host an online dinner. Invite family and friends to share a meal via a video app like Skype or FaceTime.

Connect via text and email. Be sure to use lots of emojis or gifs that emphasize physical touch, like thumbs-up or waving hands.

Talk with neighbors outside. Chat at a safe distance through a window or from a porch or backyard.

Try new outdoor group activities. Some group activities let you be with others without the risk involved in close quarters or touching. Try classes that involve physical distancing .

The bottom line

If you're feeling touch starved, you haven't sealed your fate. There are plenty of ways to beat the condition and inspire positive, affectionate touch in those around you.

End of Article

3 Surprising Ways Hugging Benefits Your Well-Being

Embracing someone can boost both your mental and physical health.

Sebastian Ocklenburg, Ph.D.

The Asymmetric Brain

Posted Dec 11, 2018

1. Hugging reduces the risk to catch a cold.

Life can be tough sometimes, and many of us have experienced that under high psychological stress, we are more likely to get sick and catch a cold or something worse. What helps us push through <u>stressful</u> periods in our lives is obviously highly individual, but for a lot of people, caring physical touch, such as a heartfelt hug, can be a great stress reliever. The interesting question is: Can it also help us be physically healthier? The answer is probably yes.

Evidence for this idea is provided in a 2015 study published in the scientific journal Psychological Science (<u>Cohen et al., 2015</u>). The authors investigated the relationship of hugging, social support, and the probability of getting sick in 404 volunteers from the Pittsburgh area. First, the volunteers were called every evening for 14 days and asked about their social relationships and whether or not they had been hugged that day. On average, participants received hugs on 68 percent of days, and there was a clear relationship that individuals who had been hugged more also felt like they received greater social support.

Now for the interesting part of the study: Some time after the phone interviews had been completed, the volunteers were invited to an isolated floor of a local hotel and were quarantined in separate rooms. The investigators then gave them nasal drops containing a virus that caused common-cold-like illnesses. Overall, 78 percent of participants got infected with the virus. Interestingly, how often somebody had been hugged clearly influenced the infection risk. Volunteers who had been hugged more had a decreased risk of infection. Moreover, among volunteers who got infected, those who had been hugged more had less severe symptoms, e.g., their noses were less stuffy. The authors concluded that hugging is an effective way to reduce stress and infection risk by conveying social support. Thus, the next time you feel like you might be getting a cold, consider hugging someone: It might be the thing that keeps you healthy.

2. **Hugging reduces your blood pressure.**

The common cold does not seem to be the only disease affected by hugging. Cardiovascular diseases are among the leading causes of death in the United States and in many other countries. One of the major risk factors for developing potentially fatal heart disease is high blood pressure. Interestingly, hugging has been suggested to reduced blood pressure, and evidence for this idea is provided in a 2005 study published in the scientific journal Biological Psychology (Light et al., 2005).

In this study, 59 women between 20 and 49 years of age who were in long-term relationships were invited to the researchers' lab together with their partners. Upon arrival, they were separated from their partners for 30 minutes, after which their partners joined them again for 10 minutes. During this period, the couples were seated on a loveseat and were encouraged to hold hands. They also watched a romantic video and were instructed to hug each other for 20 seconds at the end of the time period. After that, the partners had to leave the room, and the women had to participate in a stress test that involved giving a free speech about an event that made them feel stressed. Before, during, and after this stress test, oxytocin, the human pair bonding hormone, was measured.

The women also underwent several blood pressure measurements and had to fill out a questionnaire on how frequently they hugged their partners. The results? More frequent hugs were related to higher oxytocin levels and lower baseline blood pressure. Thus, frequent partner hugging enhances cardiovascular health and therefore potentially reduces the risk of heart disease. So the next time you leave the house and go to work, don't forget to hug your partner: It is not only good for your relationship, but also helps keep your heart healthy.

3. **Hugging can lighten up your mood, even on the worst days**.

Arguing with someone we love can leave us in a terrible mood. Hugging can make things look much brighter even in such unpleasant situations. In a recent study by <u>Murphy et al. (2018)</u>, several hundred adults were called every night for two weeks and asked about conflicts with other people in their lives, whether they felt in a good or bad mood, and whether they had received one or more hugs that day. Ninety-three percent of volunteers indicated that they had received a hug on at least one of the interview days, and 69 percent of volunteers had experienced at least one conflict with another person on one of the interview days. In general, volunteers felt better than usual on days on which they had received at least one hug, and worse on days on which they had experienced conflicts with other people. Interestingly, if they received a hug on a day in which they had also gotten into a fight with someone, the conflict appeared to lead to a smaller increase in bad mood. Moreover, hugs had a protective effect: When participants received a hug on one day and got into a fight the next day, they experienced a smaller increase in bad mood than when not having received a hug the day before. These findings suggest that hugs provide a buffer for the deleterious psychological effects that the stress caused by fighting with someone else can have on our mood. Thus, when in doubt whether to hug someone or not, as long as they feel comfortable with it, do it — it might help them (and you!) to get through the next fight a little less stressed.

References for articles

Cohen S, Janicki-Deverts D, Turner RB, Doyle WJ. (2015). Does hugging provide stress-buffering social support? A study of susceptibility to upper respiratory infection and illness. Psychol Sci, 26, 135-147.

Light KC, Grewen KM, Amico JA. (2005). More frequent partner hugs and higher oxytocin levels are linked to lower blood pressure and heart rate in premenopausal women. Biol Psychol, 69, 5-21.

Murphy MLM, Janicki-Deverts D, Cohen S. (2018). Receiving a hug is associated with the attenuation of negative mood that occurs on days with interpersonal conflict. PLoS One, 13, e0203522.

THINK ABOUT IT

Did your family give hugs when you were growing up?

_____

Who gave the best hugs?

_____

Do you hug your spouse daily?

_____

How often do you hug your children?

_____

How important is it for you to receive hugs?

_____

How hard is it for you to offer a hug to someone that has offended you?

_____

DON'T WAIT TO
ALWAYS BE THE
RECEIVER OF A HUG,
MAKE AN
INTENTIONAL EFFORT
TO HUG EVERYDAY

A Few Short Stories

The healing power of touch has been for many years the reason why some people live longer and why some heal faster than others. Several years ago, in an article written about an older couple in the state of Texas. Their story bought national attention to the medical profession. The wife had become ill and nothing the doctors did seem to be working, so they gave up trying help her. Her husband decided that along with praying for her, he would use The Power of Touch. A stunning discovery was made. The wife's health improved, and her recovery was remarkable.

Personal Story

In April 1993, I injured my right shoulder and it led to me having to have 10 major surgeries on my shoulder. All I can say is, I so thankful for the Healing Power of The Blood of Christ does work. I will try to make this story as short as I can, so you will understand the point of the story.

The injury to my shoulder was a simple act of catching a falling box from a storage closet at my place of employment at the time. The box was heavy and fell from above my head, just to give you a picture of what happened. Once I caught the box, I immediately had to place it on the floor because of the weight of the box. At that time, I did experience some pain but continued to complete my assignment. Did I feel immediate pain, yes I did, but I pushed through. When I got home, I put an ice pack on it and took some pain meds. I was able to drive to work the nest day. I worked for the next few months in pain but making it manageable. One Sunday in June 1993, the pain was so bad I had to go to the ER. When I got there and was examined, I was diagnosed as having a condition called bursitis, so it was recommended that I see a rheumatologist. I saw one on that Wednesday. He decided that I needed cortisone injections to ease the pain.

For the next three months I would receive cortisone injections to treat bursitis. The first injection didn't help much, I continued to experience pain over the next week until my next appointment. After the second injection my shoulder began to swell, it started to look like the Hunch Back of Notre Dame, literally. I could no longer rise my arm to do anything. Combing my hair, brushing my teeth, driving and any household chores were impossible at this time. It was then that I had to totally depend on my husband just to be able to move around and live life. The pain was so severe I finally went back to the doctor and told him he needed to tell me what was wrong and how do we need to proceed from here. He ordered an MRI to now look into my pain more seriously. It is so important to stand your ground when you know something is not right and also more important to not immediately accept their diagnosis. When the MRI results came back, the doctor who read it said, the spot he saw was cancer, AND IMMEDIATELY I SAY TO HIM, THAT'S A LIE AND HE NEEDED TO FIND OUT TODAY OR GET ME TO A DOCTOR THAT DOES KNOW BECAUSE I DO NOT HAVE CANCER. I

TOLD HIM I WAS NOT LEAVING THIS ROOM
UNTIL HE FINDS SOMEONE WHO KNOWS.

Well, I am happy to say he did just that. That day he got me an appointment with a doctor, the same day right around the corner from his office. I believe now was a divine appointment. I could never have imagined what the next 7 years of surgeries and therapy would bring. Not to make this a whole new book, the love and care of my husband making sure my wound was properly cared for and the way he provided hugs and encouraging words has been attributed to my healing beyond the doctor's expectations. He became an actual nurse and caregiver for me during this time. For three months he had to daily clean and dress an open incision/wound to make sure that germs did not enter. He was very meticulous about it. As a matter of fact, he did not trust that anyone else would do like he did. One day during that time he had to work overtime, and our son, Terrance had to change the bandages and clean and dress the wound. His dad told him he could do it and I must say, he did a great job.

Terrance says he did not think about what he had done until school the next day, when he became fully aware of what he had done the night before and it gave him the chills.

I am so thankful to all of our children Terrance who was 14, Trenise and Jeffrey were 4 and 6 at the time, but they were so supportive in a loving way. Always wanting to know how I was feeling and if there was something they could do to help. They gave me hugs daily but always making sure they were not hurting me.

And the rest of the story is for another book and too lengthy to go into any more details.

Just to share that loving kindness and the power of touch are important to the healing of our minds and bodies.

Think About It?

If you could write a quote about hugs, what would you say?

_____

_____

_____

_____

_____

_____

_____

_____

_____

_____

_____

_____

WHAT OTHERS SAY
ABOUT HUGS

HUG QUOTES

"The world is a mess. It seems that life gets harder on a personal level each and every day. Hug and kiss those you love every day You never know when the tragedies of this world may visit your life." – Kevin Nash

"Be a love pharmacist: dispense hugs like medicine—they are!" – Terri Guillemets

"I love meeting people, and I know it's so difficult for people to come up to me and introduce themselves, so when they do, I'll grab them and hug them. It makes their day, you know? I love that, and I get positive energy from that." – Nicola Formichetti

"Hugs and kisses are ways to express what cannot be said." – Kacie Conroy

"When you are hugging a child, always be the last one to let go. You never know how long they need it." – Unknown

"A hug is a wonderful thing. It's a marvelous gift to share. It's a grand way to say; 'I care.' A hug communicates support, security, affection, unity, and belonging. A hug shows compassion. A hug brings delight. A hug charms the senses. A hug touches the soul." – Unknown

"Sometimes a silent hug is the only thing to say." – Robert Brault

"A hug is like a boomerang - you get it back right away." ~Bil Keane, "Family Circus"

"Millions and millions of years would still not give me half enough time to describe that tiny instant of all eternity when you put your arms around me and I put my arms around you." ~Jacques Prévert

"Everybody needs a hug. It changes your metabolism." ~Leo Buscaglia

"You can't wrap love in a box, but you can wrap a person in a hug." ~Author Unknown

"I have a present for you, but I need to borrow your arms for wrapping paper." ~Author Unknown

"Hug Department: Always Open" ~Author Unknown

A hug delights and warms and charms,
that must be why God gave us arms.
~Author Unknown

"There's something in a simple hug
That always warms the heart,
It welcomes us back home
And makes it easier to part...."
~Johnny Ray Ryder, Jr "A Simple Hug"

 "No matter how hard you hug your money, it never hugs back." ~Quoted in P.S. I Love You, compiled by H. Jackson Brown, Jr.

Arm ourselves for war? No! All the arms we need are for hugging. ~Author Unknown

"I will not play at tug o' war
I'd rather play at hug o' war,
Where everyone hugs"
Instead of tugs.... ~Shel Silverstein

"A hug is a handshake from the heart." ~Author Unknown

You can't give a hug without getting a hug. ~Author Unknown

"Hugs are the universal medicine. " ~Author Unknown

"A hug is a great gift - one size fits all, and it's easy to exchange." ~Author Unknown

Happiness is an unexpected hug. ~Author Unknown

"A kiss without a hug is like a flower without the fragrance." ~Proverb

A hug is an amazing thing
It's just the perfect way
To show the love we're feeling
But can't find the words to say
~Johnny Ray Ryder, Jr., "A Simple Hug"

"If you're angry at a loved one, hug that person. And mean it. You may not want to hug - which is all the more reason to do so. It's hard to stay angry when someone shows they love you, and that's precisely what happens when we hug each other." ~Walter Anderson, The Confidence Course, 1997

There's nothing like a mama-hug. ~Terri Guillemets

A mom's hug lasts long after she lets go. ~Author Unknown

"Hugs grease the wheels of the world." ~Author Unknown

"Your hugs and kisses are like the stars that light up my life when things get dark." ~Author Unknown

"A hug is worth a thousand words." ~Author Unknown

"Every day you should reach out and touch someone. People love a warm hug, or just a friendly pat on the back." ~Maya Angelou

"Every time I think of you, it is like getting a hug from the inside out." ~Author Unknown

"Have you hugged yourself today?"~Anonymous

"A hug is two hearts wrapped in arms." ~Author Unknown

"I don't discriminate - I'm an equal-opportunity hugger."

Author Unknown

"Hugging has no unpleasant side effects and is all natural. There are no batteries to replace, it's inflation-proof and non-fattening with no monthly payments. It's non-taxable, non-polluting, and is, of course, fully refundable. " ~Author Unknown

"Hugs don't need new equipment,
Special batteries or parts -
Just open up your arms
And open up your hearts."
~Johnny Ray Ryder, Jr., "A Simple Hug"

"A hug is like a bandage to a hurting wound." ~Author Unknown

"Never wait until tomorrow to hug someone you could hug today, because when you give one, you get one right back your way .~Author Unknown

Sometimes it's better to put love into hugs than to put it into words. ~Author Unknown

A hug is the shortest distance between friends. ~Author Unknown-

"Where I live if someone gives you a hug, it's from the heart." – Steve Irwin "Getting people where they want to go, reliably and happily, can make or break their ability to succeed in a work endeavor or to hug a family member at an important moment." – Oscar Munoz

"If you're angry at a loved one, hug that person. And mean it. You may not want to hug – which is all the more reason to do so. It's hard to stay angry when someone shows they love you, and that's precisely what happens when we hug each other." – Walter Anderson

"With age, you get to a place where you don't want to knock people out. You just want to give people a hug."
– Vin Diesel

"Everbody needs a hug. It changes your metabolism."
– Leo Buscaglia

. "A hug a day keeps the demons at bay." – German Proverb

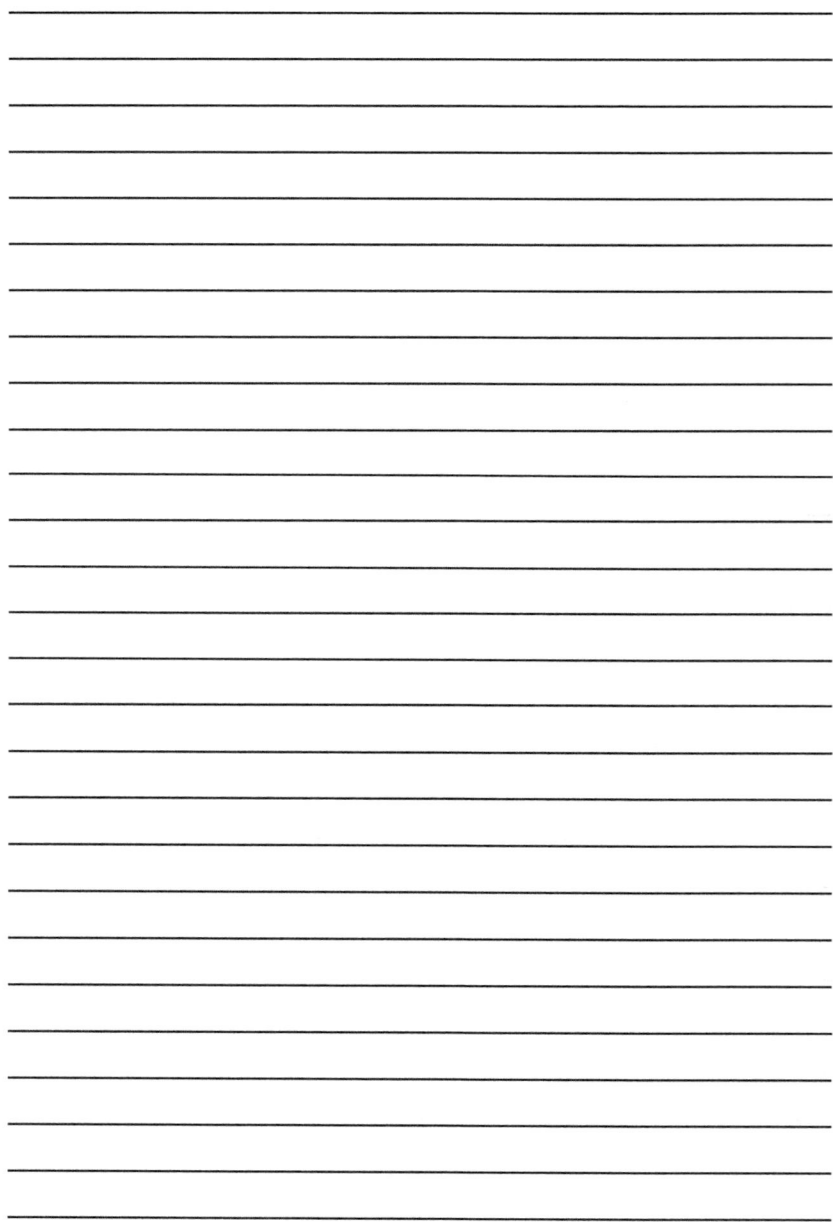

90 DAY HUG CHALLENGE

For the next ninety days keep a record of how many hugs you gave and received.

REMEMBER THE MORE HUGS YOU GIVE AWAY THE MORE HUGS YOU WILL RECEIVE.

1. GIVE HUGS TO OTHERS OFTEN BY STARTING AT HOME IF YOU LIVE WITH OTHERS.

2. Husbands intentionally hug your wives at least three times per day and make sure that by the end of ninety days she is receiving at least eight 20 second hugs from you per day.

3. Parents hug your children every day, several times per day to start and make sure it is genuine.

4. Get a massage within the next ninety days if you have a problem hugging others.

5. Greet family members with hugs at family gatherings.

6. Make it a point to give a hug to someone who has lost a loved one.

ABOUT THE AUTHOR

GWENDOLYN B. ELMORE is a wife, a mother, a friend, a singer/songwriter, an author, Certified Marriage Educator/Coach and Certified Marriage Mentor.

She is married to Eugene Elmore, an anointed man of God. They have three adult children, Terrance Patrick (Nicole), Trenise Genyetta and Jeffrey Bernard (Brittany). She is the doting grandmother of Michelle Renae, Jeremiah Patrick, Payse Frazier, Olivia Patrice and Jacob Jeffrey.

She believes that forgiveness is the key to true success in life. She also believes that hugs are important to one's health.

Follow The Marriage Educator Coach on Social Media.

WordPress Blog: http://medicministry.blog

Facebook: https://www.facebook.com/medicministry

Instagram: @themarriageeducatorcoach

www.ingramcontent.com/pod-product-compliance
Lightning Source LLC
Chambersburg PA
CBHW051707090426
42736CB00013B/2573